WIDOWED

Philip Jebb

ST. BEDE'S PUBLICATIONS
Still River, Massachusetts

Nihil obstat: Dom Illtyd Trethowan
               Censor Deputatus
Imprimatur: Dom John Roberts
               Abbot of St. Gregory's Abbey, Downside
15 May 1983

The Nihil obstat and Imprimatur are official declarations that a
book or pamphlet is free of doctrinal and moral error. No implica-
tion is contained therein that those who have granted the Nihil
obstat and Imprimatur agree with the content, opinions or state-
ments expressed.

Acknowledgments

The author and publisher wish to express their gratitude to the
following for permission to include copyrighted material in this
book:
A. D. Peters & Company for "A Tender Farewell to the World" by
Hilaire Belloc.
The relatives of the late Hilaire Belloc for various material.
"Song of Honour" reprinted with permission of Macmillan Pub-
lishing Company from *Poems* by Ralph Hodgson. Copyright 1917
by Macmillan Publishing Co., Inc., renewed 1945 by Ralph
Hodgson.
The poem by Siegfried Sassoon from *Collected Poems* of Siegfried
Sassoon. Copyright 1918, 1920 by E. P. Dutton & Co. Copyright
1936, 1946, 1947, 1948 by Siegfried Sassoon. Reprinted by per-
mission of Viking Penguin, Inc.
Scripture references from *The Holy Bible, Revised Standard Version,
Catholic Edition*, London: Catholic Truth Society, 1966.

LIBRARY OF CONGRESS CATALOGING IN PUBLICATION DATA

Jebb, Philip.
  Widowed.

  1. Widows. 2. Widowers. 3. Bereavement—Religious aspects
—Christianity. 4. Death—Psychological aspects. 5. Widows—
Religious life. 6. Widowers—Religious life. I. Title.
HQ1058.J42 1984   306.8'8   83-11160
ISBN 0-932506-30-5

Contents

Preface

This rare book of understanding and sympathy for the widowed is so good that there might well be a tendency on the part of the donor to give it to the widowed with a slight sigh of relief—as we all know a personal letter of condolence is one of the hardest to write, but the personal message is of great importance whether by letter or word of mouth. So *Widowed* must be an addition to the personal message and not a substitute, and the time of giving must be chosen carefully when it is believed and hoped that the widowed may be ready to take in not only the understanding and sympathy but also the many answers to practical problems that loom large in those early days of widowhood and can often continue long after. Dom Philip Jebb touches on many of these issues discussing them in the context of a balanced spiritual background.

The recipient reading this remarkable little book slowly, chapter by chapter through the dark nights of suffering, cannot fail to find some source of help and healing leading in time to a realization that joy will come in the morning through the demanding call of widowhood.

Joane Rittner

Foreword

A book should be its own justification, but perhaps one word of explanation would not be out of place over the poems and meditations at the end of each chapter. Those that are not attributed to anyone were written by myself either specifically for this work or else originally on some other occasion. The preponderance of quotations from Hilaire Belloc must be excused on the grounds that he was my grandfather, and I find that all too often my thoughts are clothed instinctively in his words, but with his *Tender Farewell to the World* I have taken a liberty for which I hope I will be pardoned. As for Maia, Ridalvo, Brangwen and Amoreth, who appear on page 37, I had always assumed that they were Florentines and the children of Boccaccio, but search as I may I can find them nowhere save in this verse, and there I am happy to leave them until that Great Day when we shall all meet together.

Downside Abbey   **PHILIP JEBB**

1 The Church's Widowhood

THE CHURCH IS OFTEN called the bride of Christ, and it is used with great effect in the New Testament writings of Saint Paul in his epistles and of Saint John in the Apocalypse, but it does not contain the whole story for us here and now. And Our Lord was quite clear about this, for he saw the sense in which the Church was going to be a widow. When he was asked why his disciples did not fast he replied: "Surely the bridegroom's attendants would never think of mourning so long as the bridegroom is with them. But the time will come for the bridegroom to be taken away from them and then they will fast" (Mt. 9:14). The Church has experienced a swift flash of consummation and glory as Christ came secretly, appearing from the cave in Bethlehem and returning to that beside Calvary. She saw with her own eyes that seeming defeat turned to victory, but forty days later (how could it be so swift?) she had to see her beloved depart in his visible presence, and since then has had to live and work and suffer on the strength of the Spirit within. This is our faith, which has overcome the world (1 Jn. 5:4), or rather, which is overcoming; and the process can be very hard on the way.

All men have deep within them rooted the sense of exile and of loss, and it is curious how people can deny the essential truth of the Fall as told by the Church: that we have taken a great hurt, and all the striving of Man (and of God) is toward the healing of it. The loss is so great that we cannot, most of the time, find means to express it. Perhaps Plato came as near as anyone when he spoke of all our knowledge and understanding being only explained in terms of a great and all embracing vision that we had in Paradise with God before ever we were born—and that is why, I suppose, Adam had the power to give their names to all the things he saw. A boy I knew, of deep feeling and perception, once said to me: "I suppose, if we could remember it, the horror of coming from the womb, of being born, must be far, far worse than anything death could ever do to us."

But not only are we exiled and estranged from our true home: the barriers are also up between each one of us (as again is seen in Genesis when the nakedness of Adam and Eve is recognized and clothed). We fail in our communication, in that interpenetration, which is love. We are even at rivalry over each other's good, and so hate and murder are on our hands and in our eyes. In some way we all have upon us the mark of Cain, and the blood of Jesus is upon all mankind. We have all helped to build monuments to the prophets (Lk. 11:47).

We can take this fact and process of dissolution even further, for we are not at one even within ourselves. "I cannot understand," says Saint Paul, "my own behavior. I fail to carry out the things I want to do, and I find myself doing the very things I hate" (Rom. 7:15). "*Odi et amo*," said Catullus: "I hate and I love, don't ask me how, I just know it, and it tears me in two." All the powers of modern psychology appear to be aimed at 'integrating' the person: making a living whole out of the scattered parts. And this it is right to do. But it is not within our power to do it all. So the Church, along with all mankind, feels within her a sense of failing and of loss, but she has also within her (unlike so many individuals) the consciousness of the heights achieved and of a future to be secured. She sees that final and perfect union is not within her power to command: it is that of which she has the seeds and promise within her, but the full realization is in the union with her beloved, who is Christ: who is still to come in glory.

Those, therefore, who have suffered this fearful amputation which is widowhood, who feel that they are only half their true selves; who limp and have lost their balance; who look up at each new face and do not find their searching eyes enlightened; these have their place right close to the center of this stricken world, and their life can be taken up even now into the glory which the Church proclaims. They, before most others,

stand witness to the power of love, that we
are not ourselves alone; that we must stand
in 'stretched desire'; that what was, shall be.
They, by their very loss, can share more than any
others in the victory of the Church's faith: they,
before all others can cry out for God's Kingdom
to come, for already they have so special a Communion with the Saints. Some great part of them
has gone before them: they, therefore, understand Our Lord's meaning in the words: "I am
going now to prepare a place for you, and after I
have gone and prepared you a place I shall return
to take you with me, so that where I am you may
also be" (Jn. 14:2).

Peace does not have to be made by man, it
already *is*, and man's task is to come to it. And this
is known best and deepest by those who have
fallen in love: the love is there and awaits us. God
is love, and the pains of widowhood, enfolded in
the bright light of Resurrection, are that which
can take us all to the heart of the world; their
steadfastness in the realization of having been
loved can carry the life of the world. Widows
come into their own at the Easter Vigil: "This
most holy night through which the Church
watches."

The Church is witness to all mankind, finding
within herself God's truth, and while not all
are Apostles or prophets or teachers, *all* are
witnesses to the many aspects of the one reality.

And among that cloud of witnesses the widows' place is very close to the heart of it all. It is an experience and a suffering which is immensely creative and important, if only they will let it be so. It was a widower who wrote:

> I stood in the desert, and I watched the snows
> On Aures, in their splendour from the West.
> Sahara darkened: and I thought of those
> That hold in isolation and are blest.
>
> They that in dereliction grow perfected:
> They that are silent: they that stand apart:
> They that shall judge the world as God's elected:
> They that have had the sword athwart their heart.
> *Hilaire Belloc*

O God, you who brought life to the silent desert of uncreated space, and bring gain out of every seeming loss, grant to those of your children who have lost the bright light of their love and the touch of their companion, an openness to what is eternally alive in you, that all creation may from their lives draw strength.

2 Death

DEATH, HOWEVER HE COMES, always seems to lessen those who have to witness his coming: it is not just that we have lost the person who dies. It is more than this: our own selves are threatened and something goes out from us with the one who dies. When we mourn the dead a great deal of our sorrow is for us who remain, for we are brought face to face with what we are, with the great alternative within us: there is always the possibility of extinction.

This body of ours has to die, we know. It has not got the power within it to be immortal, but its life is a sign and a symbol of the fullness of life to which we can come, and death is equally a sign and a symbol of the awfulness of ultimate failure. It is a sign and a symbol of what evil is, what sin is.

God calls us into being out of nothing: we are made up of nothing and his creative Word. He gives to us the power to say *Yes* to his creative act (2 Cor. 1:19), and by this enables us to come to a real share in his ultimate bliss. This must of its nature be a free act on our part, for this life is simply love (for that is what God is) and therefore we must be free to reject it if we so will. And that rejection (which is the ultimate sin) is most fully symbolized by death.

But, of course, when someone dear to us dies there is the agony of loss; all the gates of communication seem closed; direction is snatched away from our lives; warmth is lost; there is not that beside us to which all our sensibility has learnt to turn. But this is the wound Our Lord set out to heal: it is here that Death loses his victory, for the assertion of Resurrection is that nothing is ever finally lost.

Every passing moment is a death: the present is constantly dying into the past: we can never hold, and to try to is illusion. Every shake of the kaleidoscope means death to the beauty of the previous pattern. We have not that quality of God to be all-at-once, but so much of our nature seems to call out in anguish as it recognizes this lack.

But there is a further invasion of death in our lives when we come up against the blank wall of meaninglessness within us: when we quarrel with the one we love; when we see what has to be done and will not do it; when we betray; when what we have worked and strained after and desired is snatched from us and broken before our eyes; when the whole world is pointless, and makes of us an object. Death is the final invasion of nothingness. If we have not felt any of this, then we have not yet fully lived.

What then is Christ's answer? To wrap a strong cocoon around us of surety in the resurrection? To say, However bad things are now, it *will* work out in the end? To return to the past or look forward to the future?

No. On the cross Our Lord showed us God in the final agony of naked frustration and nothingness and abandonment, and then showed that this is a *price*: the price of Creation's coming from nothing. And if creation is to come home to its infinite creator it must pass right through this nothingness to be wholly rid of it, to be confirmed in existence. This is what Our Lord meant when he said: "Unless a grain of wheat falls into the earth and dies, it remains alone; but if it dies it bears much fruit. He who loves his life loses it, and he who hates his life in this world will keep it for eternal life" (Jn. 12:24). This is what Saint Paul meant when he said that we die continually (1 Cor. 15:31), and that death is at work in us, but life in you (2 Cor. 4:11).

The more real, therefore, that we are, the more of existence we have in us, the more terrible death is, for there is so much more at risk. But the more fully we 'live' this death, the stronger our real life and capacity. If we are to complete the fullness of our life we have to live to the uttermost the reality of this choice—to be or not to be—and then to come down wholly on the side of affirmation and being and outgoing love.

Some people would say that *pain* is a little death, and there is a sense, of course, in which this is true, for the hurt always reminds us of our limited condition: in some ways we are coming up against a wall. As Proust says: "Pain is the one true Doctor we obey." But in a much more important sense Our Lord has shown that pain is only deadly if we succumb to it and *allow* it to be deadly. I want to look at this in more detail in Chapter 13, but for the moment I would want to say that the true message of Our Lord's Passion is that pain is the working out of life. Indeed there have been times when I have really only known that I was alive because I could feel God's love in pain—as life comes back into frost-bitten hands with excruciating agony, or as love tortures us after a withdrawal into the desert of no human relationships. That is why Saint Paul says: "While we live we are always being given up to death for Jesus' sake, so that the life of Jesus may be manifested in our mortal flesh" (2 Cor. 4:11).

Those therefore who live, but who have Death most intimately bound up with their lives, can come through this to the real power of the Resurrection, and in great measure carry and lead us all. Blake was right to say that joys impregnate and sorrows bring forth.

> Wonder is so sudden a gift:
> Straight from the shooting star,
> Or slow dark fishes in pools;

Found in the bursting, toe stretching exertions of
    babes
And the beard's old furrowed ground.

What a kingdom you display
As you call me to delight:
What generosity is mine
As I survey the infinite world: yours to me.
Here is fruit for all time;
Here is a way picked out with full joy;
Here means without end
Masters a freedom full.

And Death?
Impossible!
And yet:
In Arcadia Ego.

Oh, the break and the bruise;
The tottered reign
Tumbled in dark confusion
Satanic and shrieking.

Where now the certitudes of joy?
Does Nothing prevail?

Ah, the lie
Given and received.
Must all be broken?
Has wonder fallen to a sum?

Only so the path to Resurrection,
When Death has been chewed over,
Met with and faced,
Farmed right through.
But the glory from that encounter braved

What man can tell?

Come Lord.

Jesus, you wept over the death of Lazarus, and felt abandoned in the face of your own; give therefore to us who must live with this searching spear deep in our hearts, the all conquering power which draws all things to yourself, and which is your risen life. Amen.

3 Resurrection

CHRISTIANITY IS REGARDED by so many people as a moral code, as a way of doing things: "Love thy neighbor as thyself," or "Turn the other cheek," or "Greater love hath no man than this, that he lay down his life for his friends." But this is not the essential Christian message: the thing that Our Lord constantly laid stress upon, and demanded at all times was Faith. In the first instance this was a simple and unconditional faith in him ("Who else can we turn to? For you have the words of eternal life" [Jn. 6:68]). But by the end of his mission on earth his followers were clear about the content of their faith, they saw what was unique about him and the message they had to proclaim. They saw as the prime facts to be believed the Incarnation, and the Resurrection. All else in Christianity follows from these. God has become man, we are freed from our sins (whose wages are death), and beyond the death of the body is a resurrection, to a share in the divine life of God.

It is in the light of our faith in this series of dogmas (or teachings) that we live by our moral code and order our actions towards a clearly recognized end—this is what is meant by Our Lord's saying that he is the Way, the Truth and the Life (Jn. 14:6).

But having looked at Death, let us now look a little more closely at what is meant by this teaching of resurrection. First, let us note the insistence on its being the resurrection of the body. This has difficulties, but I think the point to be made here is that we are in the first instance the sum of all that we have experienced, and all our experience has been in the body if not through it. The body is always changing (even as we cut our hair, or take a cup of tea after donating a pint of blood) but the experiences have in them an element of the unchanging and of the eternal: we pack them away in memory and in scars, and in all the other stable forms of our development. But essentially all our past experience lives only because we live. And therefore by resurrection we are freed from the agony of the passing moment, the awareness of things racing beyond recall. Nothing that is real is now lost. And I am careful to say *what is real*, because evil and failure and pain are not real in this sense: they are the threat and the destruction of what is real and good, and therefore they do not have standing and resurrection. They are the gaps that are to be swallowed up in victory when God becomes all in all (1 Cor. 15:28 and 55). Therefore *in the end* Keats was wrong to talk of Beauty that must die, and of Joy whose hand is ever at his lips, bidding adieu. For all the time, as we grow in the richness of experience, we are not losing those experiences, but storing them up for our future glory, and not just simply our own glory, but everyone else's as well as ours, as we come to share in the one single life of Christ, and not only are we simply preserving them, but we are, by the very fact of living them generously, increasing our capacity for life given and received. The more we live and love the more we are capable of this, the more we can give to others what has been given to us and the more we can receive from others. And so do we build up that one great good, which is God's life among men, man's life in God.

Of course there must be regret at not having in living presence with us now the pinnacles of joy and companionship which once we had, but this is where we overcome the world, this is the victory: our faith in the triumphant resurrection. Every particle of joy and fulfillment and achievement to which we give ourselves, far from being lost, is to be enhanced by its interaction with all else in the staggering and unimaginable wealth of the whole of experienced creation.

And since it would appear that by its very nature our spirit enlivens a body, in the Resurrection we will be 'embodied' again. But the *form* of it we do not know, since in this passing life the body is too full of imperfections and limitations at any particular moment for it to be the lasting home of the spirit through eternity. But that which we have seen of beauty and glory in those we love must surely be confirmed and continue to shine through: we will have no difficulty, but only surpassing joy in recognizing and holding the beloved so long parted from our eyes and arms.

And there is further thought here, that as we have in store for us this resurrection in our own right by virtue of our faith in Christ, so does all the finite creation that we have known and loved attain to resurrection by virtue of ours. It has an ultimate fulfillment dependent on ours: when I have seen and gloried in a sunset, that experience becomes a part of me and goes with me forever, and so also with those animals in which I have taken joy: those stars which have talked to me at night, great winds, and the waves upon the shore. All these will come to triumph in me and with me. And indeed, when I begin to think upon this with the certitudes of faith given by the Church, I see more clearly how the whole colossal drive of creation is a single outpouring of God, and since God knows and loves it, I cannot see how any of its true reality can ever be lost.

Our power in Christ, therefore, is to be able to inject this whole creation with the thrill of resurrection: to carry to each and every encounter, through each and every moment of our lives, this fullness of life borne upon faith, bursting out into love never to be lost.

I heard the universal choir,
The Sons of Light exalt their Sire
With universal song...
I heard the hymn of being sound
From every well of honour found
In human sense and soul:
The song of poets when they write
The testament of Beautysprite
Upon a flying scroll,
The song of painters when they take
A burning brush for Beauty's sake
And limn her features whole—

The song of men divinely wise
Who look and see in starry skies
Not stars so much as robins' eyes,
And when these pale away
Hear flocks of shiny pleiades
Among the plums and apple trees
Sing in the summer day—

. . .

The song of lovers—who knows how
Twitched up from place and time
Upon a sigh, a blush, a vow,
A curve or hue of cheek or brow,
Borne up and off from here and now
Into the void sublime!

. . .

The song of each and all who gaze
On Beauty in her naked blaze,
Or see her dimly in a haze,
Or get her light in fitful rays

And tiniest needles even...
The everlasting pipe and flute
Of wind and sea and bird and brute,
And lips deaf men imagine mute
In wood and stone and clay.

. . .

I heard it all, each, every note
Of every lung and tongue and throat,
Ay, every rhythm and rhyme
Of everything that lives and loves
And upward, ever upward moves
From lowly to sublime!
Earth's multitudinous Sons of Light,
I heard them lift their lyric might
With each and every chanting sprite
That lit the sky that wondrous night
As far as eye could climb!
I heard it all, I heard the whole
Harmonious hymn of being roll
Up through the chapel of my soul
And at the altar die,
And in the awful quiet then
Myself I heard, Amen, Amen,
Amen I heard me cry!
I heard it all and then although
I caught my flying senses, Oh,
A dizzy man was I!
I stood and stared; the sky was lit,
The sky was stars all over it,
I stood, I knew not why,
Without a wish, without a will,
I stood upon that silent hill

And stared into the sky until
My eyes were blind with stars and still
I stared into the sky.

from the Song of Honour, *by Ralph Hodgson*

Dear Lord, there are sorrows and failings in this life of ours, but you have given us the taste of such wonder and joy, and through your Resurrection we have the confidence that nothing real can ever be lost; so give us always that strength in your love which will let us bring from the depths of our own experiences the fullness of your creation, so that in the great reunion of us all we may each bring a rich store for the infinite bliss of us all.

4 Unsupported

WHATEVER THE QUALITIES of the relationship in any particular marriage, whatever the strains or difficulties, there is always companionship: there is support given and received. Two beings conjoined give support each to the other, and in the ideal arrangement of true mutual support the more one leans the more the other needs to also: in receiving support we give it: in giving support we receive it. Action and reaction are a single nexus, and men were well aware of it long before Newton worked out the sum of it.

Now the removal of support is catastrophic: a single stone can stand and stand: it is of itself. But when stones are bent into an arch each holds a dynamic place, essential to the stability of the whole, and with the removal of any single component the whole must collapse. And of sticks and stones (which break our bones) there is nothing more to be said, but in life there is a further chapter to the story: here all growth seems to come only as the result of removing the supports.

When the companion of our life is gone we are faced with the most fearsome call: all sharing seems at an end, decisions are like lone bullets through the air, pleasures go unshared and are halved, while sorrows and assaults are doubled. And this enters into every aspect of widowed life, and if they are enumerated here it is not so much to tell the bereaved of what they are aware they are suffering, but rather to be a pointer for those who have not suffered this, that they may be more realistic and imaginative in helping such people, and to help any who have been widowed, and who read this book, to realize that its considerations are not wholly out of touch with flesh and blood reality.

Those who are widowed sleep alone, and there is no comfort in the night. Perhaps worse: they wake alone, and no added strength comes with returning consciousness. If pain of mind or body takes sleep from them they have no human recourse. The sexual gift, hitherto so much a part of life, must now suddenly be denied. Often they will have to eat alone and feel the pointlessness of making any effort to prepare a meal only for themselves; so often they will return to an empty house without a companion and with no one to welcome them (even harder at night and after a party). And being alone they are less easy to invite to parties, less easy to 'balance' or to 'fit in'; and entering a room with all the others already there, they have no respite from making all the going themselves: that one, constant secret face is no longer there giving point to all the others.

It was Hilaire Belloc in his widowhood who wrote:

> There will be no meeting of eyes nor any blessing
> after the run.
> The lips are still, and the hand has ceased from
> caressing.
> There is nothing more to be done.

This is where Death comes to us at his most nearest: this is the dividing of Spirit.

And yet.

What did our Lord say to his frightened Apostles on their last night together? "It is to your advantage that I go away, for if I do not go away the Counselor will not come to you" (Jn. 16:7). If they clung always to his physical, visible presence, they could never grow up to the strength and reality of the Spirit within them. If always we were carried in our mothers' arms we would never learn to walk: we only walk ourselves when we take away the support of one of the two feet on which we so securely stand. It is only Death himself who can fling us 'beyond Auxerre.' He is the final launcher: he knocks away the chocks that keep us so steady above the sweet boundless sea.

In the act of removal all is immediately appalling emptiness, panic and confusion (much worse than simply having been always alone), but once it is truly under way we can begin to catch a glimpse of Our Lord's great claim to be making all things new (Apoc. 21:5): we are not falling away from those whose life made one being with ours, but rather we are growing into an infinite opportunity of interaction with all else that exists.

A young Hindu once asked the oldest and wisest of teachers that he knew what it was that held up the world and stopped it from falling, and that sage replied that the world was carried by an elephant, and the young man went off content and relieved.

And yet? And yet?

So the next year he was back to ask what supported the elephant, and was told it was a turtle...

And now our own wise men have taken even the stable ground from beneath our feet, and have melted our too solid flesh into whirling forces lost in the lonely seas of space. And yet? And yet?

Why yes, it moves, and it is better that it should go.

A psalm of David: to the Choirmaster, according to Lilies

Save me, O God!
For the waters have risen to my neck.
I sink deep in mire,
where there is no foothold;

I have come into deep waters,
and the flood sweeps over me.
I am weary with my crying;
my throat is parched.
My eyes grow dim with waiting for my God.
Let not those who hope in thee
be put to shame through me,
O Lord God of hosts;
let not those who seek thee
be brought to dishonour through me,
O God of Israel.
For it is for thy sake
that I have borne reproach,
that shame has covered my face.
I have become a stranger to my brethren,
an alien to my mother's sons.

But as for me, my prayer is to thee, O Lord.
At an acceptable time, O God,
In the abundance of thy steadfast love answer me;
with thy faithful help
rescue me from sinking in the mire;
let me be delivered from my enemies
and from the deep waters.
Let not the flood sweep over me,
or the deep swallow me up,
Or the pit close its mouth over me.

Answer me, O Lord,
for thy steadfast love is good;
according to thy abundant mercy turn to me.
Hide not thy face from thy servant;
for I am in distress.
Make haste to answer me.

I looked for pity,
but there was none;
and for comforters,
but found none.
I am afflicted and in pain:
Let my salvation, O God, set me on high.

I will praise the name of God with a song;
I will magnify him with thanksgiving.

You who seek God,
let your hearts revive.
For the Lord hears the needy
and does not despise his own that are in bonds.

Let heaven and earth praise him,
the seas, and everything that moves therein.
For God will save Zion
and rebuild the cities of Judah.
And his servants shall dwell there and possess it,
the children of his servants shall inherit it,
and those who love his name shall dwell in it.

Psalm 68

O God, you carry us all in your hand: you are
the ground of our being. Give me faith in your
upholding power, with your aid let me leap over
the wall.

5 The Children

BUT IN BEREAVEMENT the children are a support even if there are complications: they are the living signs of the shared life of love; by the urgency of their incompleteness they carry all with them. They are life assured. For the moment they are immortal.

How children will react to death depends enormously on their age and upbringing: the very young will really only feel the loss by proxy. They will share in the misery and shock of those around simply because it is there. But those who are older can feel the immediate loss (though not usually the numbing shock of the widow) and in some obscure way (deep down, and rarely made explicit) they can hold the survivor in some way responsible for the death, which can be a great harshness to bear, but they must not be blamed for this: it is but one step from that guilt we share with Adam and Cain. They must be helped in these straits, not goaded further.

If the children have reached their later teens they will begin to shoulder the responsibilities which the gap leaves unfulfilled. In a sense they are doing this before their time. But it must be so, and only so will they make up for the loss and wound they have suffered. They will make mistakes, as do all the inexperienced (as indeed the experienced often enough), but they must not be deterred by this, rather it must become a common search for the new pattern of shared existence. If it is their father they have lost, they will have to make for themselves so much of discipline and vision; if it is their mother, gentleness, warmth and intuition.

The widow cannot share with her children all her sorrow because (if for no other reason) it is they who are her continuing joy. There is of course the danger and temptation (especially for the widow) to lean too much upon the children and to find it all the more impossible to let them go, and this is a temptation to selfishness which can be disguised by so much of good intention, and buried by so much of inward looking pain. Children cannot simply become a substitute for the relationship now lost, but they must be brought into her sorrow and loss to the extent that this is possible to both sides, for otherwise the children will fail to come to terms with a reality to which they have a right. And for the same reason, and accordiing to their capacity, they must be made aware of the changed circumstances and responsibilities of the future, not to make of these things a burden, but again because reality is the best of nurses and teachers. They

must *all* be brought to see how death is a gateway, and that all that happens is always an opportunity that can further the creative act of God,
and that in their loss they are to concentrate not
on the bereavement but on how they have been
brought still closer together as a family. They
must walk safely and confidently in the realm of
prayer, coming to realize that their dead parent is
still part of them, indeed, more so than before;
that he or she still watches over them, still cares
for them, and has now more power and strength
to help simply because they are in the realms of
everlasting light where all we love is always dear,
and where full realization of the totality brings
together the scattered pieces of our still imper-
fect world. They are to be prayed *to* as much as *for*.
They now share as completely as it is possible to
in God's creative parenthood. They are now fore-
runners who bring with them (if a moment later)
all that he has and is.

Children can walk easily in these realms if only
they are led to them joyously and firmly, and
once they have breathed that quintessential air
their strength is of another order.

And for orphans especially, I think, has the
story of the finding in the Temple been preserved
in the Gospels. Jesus, when he was twelve, first
reached, as it seems to me, some proper inkling at
the human level of his true nature (for his human
nature had to grow and develop in the same way

as yours and mine: he had to learn to walk and talk, read and write, how to make a table or chair. Being God made no difference to the conditions of human development in the mind and body). And this realization to which he came in the twelfth year of his was of God his father. He acted on it simply and directly, but in his condition unrealistically. And when he was found three days later by Mary and Joseph he went back with them to his earthly dwelling to grow yet more in wisdom and stature before God and men. In a sense he was taken away from his true home, from the human presence of his true father, centered on the Temple. And yet in no true sense was he a loser: he gained in wisdom and stature before God and men: to know that his true and heavenly father was beyond the reach of his mortal eyes and outstretched hands could have been only a strength and inspiration and goal leading to the infinity of his fulfillment. And yet how hard and bleak and meaningless could have been that moment of submission if he could have chosen to let it be so.

> And a woman who held a babe against her bosom said, Speak to us of Children.
> And the Prophet said:
> Your children are not your children.
> They are the sons and daughters of Life's longing for itself.
> They come through you but not from you,

And though they are with you yet they belong not
   to you.
You may give them your love but not your
   thoughts,
For they have their own thoughts.
You may house their bodies but not their souls,
For their souls dwell in the house of tomorrow,
   which you cannot visit, not even in your dreams.
You may strive to be like them, but seek not to
   make them like you.
For life goes not backward nor tarries with yester-
   day.
You are the bows from which your children as
   living arrows are sent forth.
The archer sees the mark upon the path of the
   infinite, and He bends you with His might that
   His arrows may go swift and far.
Let your bending in the Archer's hand be for
   gladness;
For even as He loves the arrow that flies, so He
   loves also the bow that is stable.

               from The Prophet *by Kahlil Gibran*

Jesus, you walked the earth for our salvation
and journeyed far from your Father's side; grant
to those of us who have lost the presence of our
parents the grace to keep our eyes always on our
true home, where they now live with you for
ever and ever, and from where they look down on
us and wait for us with all the love of heaven.

6 Weeping

MAN IS UNIQUE in all creation both in his tears and in his laughter. No other creature has them, nor does the creator. Tears are man's own baptism: we are born with them, and we pass them to other eyes at our death. And between those two gates of life tears are meant to be a cleanser and a healer: their gentle salt purifies and preserves.

It is customary in our society to attribute tears more to women than to men, and even to regard them in a grown man as simply a sign of weakness. But I would think he was an impoverished man who could not weep or never would. There is nothing shameful about tears, unless they never stop or unless they are entirely inward looking. Even Our Lord could weep over Jerusalem and the dead Lazarus, and this last even though he well knew the glory of God which he was immediately to reveal. He could feel the ineffable pathos of creation and was in tune with its groanings in its longing to be set free (Rom. 8:22).

Tears then are a release and a benison, and in our loss, and in memory of our loss, we may well weep. We are right to recognize Virgil's *lachrymae rerum* (how all things are full of tears), for they call upon and open up so much of experience. For the widowed in the first instance there is the realization of loss and the agony this holds, but also there can be fear for the agonies and pains and burdens (unshared) of the future; and beyond fear can be anger at the wrongs felt to be done against us. But beyond anger again can come the tears of remorse at the weight of what might have been at our hands if only we had been truer, if only we had been braver, if only...if only.... And beyond all these? There is the sudden stab of beauty still retained and the whole heaven of ineffable desires.

For all of these tears are a true language, and can dissolve these pains into something much higher, and therefore the psalmist was right to desire the Lord to preserve them (Ps. 55). Sometimes they can be shared, sometimes they must be alone. But they are not that spring within us welling up to everlasting life (Jn. 4:14), they cannot be that by which we live. Niobe learnt one of the great lessons when she stopped weeping to eat and drink. Her tears did not then become a mockery, and eating was not a betrayal. It is, I suppose, our glory that our life at present is an interweaving of great multiplicity, and it is only through the infinite variety of its components that we can hope to come to the simplicity of God, who in all his glory does not forget this Vale of Tears through which he passed.

Did you, my poor one, weep on Winter's hill,
Dreading the fearsome cold of landscape bare?
And as the questing wind went out to kill
Stirring the waves, and deaf to any care
Did gray salt spray of ever lifting seas
Hammer less harshly at the castle's sand?
Was there no answer to your failing pleas
As urgent waters ate the recumbent land?

But restless Ocean lays the rocks anew,
Adding the marvel of a fossil's form.
The sap will soon our darling woods renew
And bring us glory from the dying storm.
Those tears that spring from keenly mourning eyes
Flow down for you to streams in Paradise.

O God, you have given to man alone of all
creation the gift of tears; grant to those who
mourn a cleansing through their sorrow, that
they may find in you that which they have for the
moment lost, and also the spring welling up to
everlasting life.

7   Loneliness and Solitude

OUR SOCIETY TENDS to make everything of company and to set no store by solitude, which it can only think of as loneliness. But these two are very different. Loneliness is indeed terrible, and is one of the very real evils, of our age especially. It is the absence of communion, the lack of communication, it is the self inadequate on its own; it is a deadening thing. But of solitude we do not see enough. And so fearful are the pains of loneliness that we think that to be alone is to be lonely. But it is not so simple.

The philosophers say that a person cannot develop, or begin to know itself as a person, except in relation to other persons: the true work of a person is interaction with another person. And this is true enough. Adam may have given Eve her name, but he was less than half fulfilled before he heard her call him by his, whether it was first thought up by him or by her or by God. But for all that, we do not simply stand in relation to others: we have that in us (we *are* that) which cannot as yet, and in this world, be simply communicated.

This inner realm where we can only walk alone

can be very frightening and seem very impoverished even when we are conscious of it at all, and
nearly all our contemporary culture is urging us
to forget it altogether. All the time we skim over
the outer face of things with celerity if not with
grace more than half convinced that if we stopped
to think of how we did it we would sink, and that
the consequences of *that* would be disastrous.

But if in fact we sink what do we find if not that
which is our base? And what is our base if not
God? This is where dwells that hound of Heaven
which the poet Francis Thompson fled over so
many arches of the years. This is that still small
voice that Elias found at the mouth of the cave on
Horeb (1 Kgs. 19:13). This is the spot Augustine
reached with his mother at Ostia when all the
world grew silent (*Confessions*, book 9). This is that
silent earth from which alone can any fruitful-
ness appear (Mk. 4:28).

If there is no solitude in our lives we are without depth, and the seed that fell on rocky ground
soon withered, for all its swift beginnings (Mt.
13:5). Our Lord before he launched out upon his
public career spent forty days alone in the desert,
and all through the hurly-burly of the ensuing
years he would take himself off alone at night
to pray when he had great business ahead (like
naming the Apostles or gathering strength for
the Passion), or when he needed renewal after
dismissing the crowds.

This in a very real sense is to break through beyond this present life: it is to outmarch Death and get beyond his bourn. This is a living sleep from which the Beauty will arise. It is here that we can fulfill the command of the Oracle at Delphi to know ourselves. Of course we must work while the day lasts (Jn. 9:4), but so much of what we do is noise and distraction and is little different from Maia, Ridalvo, Brangwen, Amoreth

> In Mountain-guarded gardens vainly gay,
> Wasting the irrecoverable breath
> Seeking to lose in play
> The fixed, majestic questioning eyes of death
> By turning theirs away.
>
> *Hilaire Belloc*

We need that questioning, and when Death has taken our beloved we need the answer too. Therefore in Rome in my youth I was not moved by anything as much as by that little retreat of Hadrian's set in the middle of its little round pool of water. Here alone could he find his soul away from the multitudinous business of Empire. And look at Julian of Norwich: shut away alone in her cell, knowing no letter, to read or write, and yet what height and depth to her revelations of divine love worked out in no lonely solitude!

When we are young we probably are not strong enough for much solitude, and Saint Benedict was wise to see that in spite of his own experience the monk is only ready to live in the

desert alone after he has learnt the discipline of
life in the community. In widowhood there will
inevitably be periods alone which were not there
before. But do not see these as simply an aching
void, as an underlining of the sense of loss. They
can become the gateway to your garden: they are
the way to all true strength, they are that from
which you go out to bring new life to our glitter-
ing and pleasant but dangerous and wholly change-
ful world. Solomon has told us (1 Kgs. 8:12) how
God has set his sun in the heavens, but has said
that he himself would dwell in thick darkness,
and thus does he underline God's solitude that is
not a loneliness; and now with the full revelation
of the Trinity in Unity we can no longer have
reason to be afraid of God the alone.

> Pure silence drops from heaven
> Only when the heart is still.

> Alone, alone, my soul,
> come to the unending centre:
> be drenched
> by the desert's single eye.

> Look out across those mists
> sheeting the peopled world at dawn.

> Remember the fenlands:
> dark lonely soil
> with solitude complete
> between the treeless dykes.

> The quiet at home

with only the even ticking of the clock
and sparrows under the eaves,
noisily selfish to the last.

Here is deep calm
from the rippling pressures of the world.

Here drink,
and find the welling fount within
where you can meet
full surcease of violence
and God's enfolding arm.

Here secrets
from before the everlasting hills.

Find strength
for all the business that must follow.
Your garden is enclosed.

Dear God,
One, living and true,
Through your Son you have shown us the
infinite life of your three persons;
Grant to us who feel the fearful threat
of loneliness
A thirst for your strong solitude,
Where, being alone with the Alone
We may be embraced by you, the All in all.

8   Changed Circumstances and Money

WITH DEATH, PARTICULARLY of the husband, circumstances almost inevitably appear reduced: in addition to the chasm of personal impoverishment, material pressures will almost immediately begin to close in. There will in a great many cases just simply be a lot less money, and fewer prospects for the future, and after so very few days much less social intercourse (the 'unattached female' is not so easy to 'fit in'). At the very moment when one's worries are increased and multiplied one finds that they must be borne unshared: it is in the loss of a husband that his strength and support and steadying influence appear as most needed; while the loss of a wife can bring a coldness and lack of vivacity that she alone could counteract. The result can be complete paralysis.

But we are not simply the slaves of our environment and circumstances unless we let ourselves be: in *any* situation in which we find ourselves it is possible to further the creative purpose of God, and sudden widowhood is no exception.

First, let us realize the necessity of moving with measured tread: we cannot rebuild Rome in a day, and it will take time to map out the narrower bounds of our lessened world. But let us go at it steadily under the hand of God, who made us, and through it all still loves us, and who guides us safely to complete and unutterable fulfillment. We must begin to take stock of our new reality: learn the creative solace of work, the comforting feel of reality in that work.

In the immediate crash there will be many signs of sympathy and many generous offers of help, and these should be accepted for what they are, and used while they still have living force. And this does not mean that we can simply be carried by them, or rest on them. They should be directed towards a purpose: used as a means towards *independence from sympathy*. Get those who can, and are willing, to help you in finding an occupation, if this is needed, in getting a new source of income if *this* is needed. Get help, from those whose judgment you trust, in assessing the whole situation in which you find yourself: the immediate needs, the future probabilities. Get help in the *assessment*, but on more than the absolutely immediate things make your own independent judgment and decision: do not allow yourself to be paralyzed or to be taken over. But on the other hand do not make decisions until they need to be—which does not mean putting them off until the last minute, but leave them until you are as far as possible in a balanced state of mind to make them: do not sell your house within a month, or change the children's school, or get all your available money tied up in some friend's business from which it will be very difficult to extricate it.

Start towards making a new pattern of life out of what you now judge to be your present resources and limits, and make even of this a living process: see (and live with the sight) that the flower must fade, the seed must die. But it cannot be said too often that there is life in the dying. Life is here as well as hereafter: indeed it is hereinafter. We know that for those who love God *all* things work together for good (Rom. 8:28). If we really live and believe this then we can never be poor. Riches are always and everywhere at hand. The answer to the call for courage and faith that Death evokes brings always an immeasurable reward and freedom. We will let Saint Paul say it again: "We are afflicted in every way, but not crushed; perplexed, but not driven to despair; persecuted, but not forsaken; struck down, but not destroyed; always carrying in the body the death of Jesus, so that the life of Jesus may also be manifested in our bodies. For while we live we are always being given up to death for Jesus' sake, so that the life of Jesus may be manifested in our mortal flesh" (2 Cor. 4:8-11).

When God made gold
He gave it so fairly:
Some heavy and soft and deep in the earth;

Hard for the miner
Groping and picking the long veins through.
And then the so rough journey
To the winter of man's bleak avarice.
It must bend to the hammer,
Melt to the fire,
Yet gleam never lost.
But oh, the weight of it.
Fool that I was,
Heavy burdened and held.

By Mine and Yours
The world is torn in two.

But now look to the light:
Light light of the world,
Infinitesimally spread.
Pollen's dust,
Drangonfly's wings,
Corn and the summer of youth.
Butterflies carry it,
Water will borrow it,
Autumn can lavish it,
The sun will lend it
(Stars in the night:
dawn's clouds);
We can behold it
But hold it?

Not thus have we held
Since Adam rebelled.
Not as of yore
Not from a mine.
But the hours go brightly,
Spread ever lightly.

Weight is a break,
Light is a spring.
So be not held
But behold
Dearest gold.

Mary, you were the Mother of God and angels talked with you, but you knew the stark poverty of Bethlehem, the uprooting of the flight into Egypt, and the loss of your husband and your Son; all this you accepted as the handmaid of the Lord, and we pray to you that we may use you as our model and guide in our own deep losses, that you may be our mother too.

9   Freedom and Service

SAINT PAUL SAYS (1 Cor. 7) that the unmarried are free to attend to the service of the Lord, and that it is a good thing for widows to remain in that state. This goes very much against the temper of our age and is far from being a statement valid for all circumstances or for all people (in fact he tells Timothy on another occasion [1 Tm. 5:14] that younger widows should marry again). But let us look for a moment at what is positive in it, and realize that widowhood does not have to be simply more or less of an aching void. The loss of the immediate focal point of life can be the chance to raise one's eyes to the further horizons. From being so concentrated, attention can now be all the more powerful in its general sweep. A widow can open out into a larger field with much more assurance than many others: all the depth of her past experience can now be brought into play, and she could well show powers of understanding and sympathy, at least, which go beyond those of the average priest in *his* unmarried state. And these are powers that the world stands at all times in need of.

The unmarried are free. This does not mean

they have no ties, no calls upon their time and
energy and attention. We should not see it as
freedom *from*, but freedom *for*. Freedom means
the ability to develop and grow without restraint.
This has very little, if anything, to do with choice,
as so many seem to think. Indeed, I would say
that free will, as such, was a limitation: an
unavoidable limitation given our nature and circumstances, and one which is the mark of our
great power to respond to the love of God, but a
limitation for all that, for to have the ability to
reject God's offer of love (for that is what is
involved in the call of man's limited nature to the
divine life) is a terrifying lack when seen beside
God's *necessity* to be and to love. In heaven we are
totally free and quite beyond the realms of
choice.

Freedom in this life does not mean there will be
no pain, but that *through* the pain life is con-
structive. When Our Lord said that he had come
not to be served but to serve he was showing one
aspect of his freedom. The person who can serve
another is free, and it is a freedom none can take
from him. How much more to be pitied are those
who cannot bring themselves to the service of
others, for if we have no one to serve we have no
one to love, and if we have no one to love where is
our freedom? Where is our life?

The real slavery is the selfishness of sin (Rom.
6:16), for if we are imprisoned in our own self-

ishness there is nothing to take us outside our tiny single-centered selves, and all creation narrows down to this single point, and all that is beyond our reach can only tantalize, and all within frustrates.

But the widow can increasingly launch out beyond her former scope, and can take Mary, the mother of God for her model: she who before all others has built up the life of the world and known every basic human experience (save the guilt of sin). From her tiny narrow circle she has won the title of Co-redeemer. And yet her immediate sphere of influence in an obscure village on the last edge of the Roman Empire must have appeared utterly negligible. We do not see Mary *doing* a great deal in the Gospels, but at the crucial points she is *there*, and she is available. Her reaction to Gabriel's Annunciation was not the effect of effortless innocence, but the fruit of already mature prayer; her Visitation to Elizabeth shows her practical good sense and loving concern once the need arose for them; there is no sign of anything but serenity in the stable-Nativity; Simeon shows how she went to her martyrdom of suffering with eyes wide open; the Finding of Jesus in the Temple (after what agonies endured for those three days) showed that she accepted her responsibilities to the uttermost, and that her authority was looked to and accepted by her Son; the Marriage Feast at Cana shows that she could precipitate, anticipate, God's 'Time' without even petition: simply by looking. During his three short years of overflowing activity she was not far away, it seems (Mt. 12:46), even though a selfish mother (and she a widow) could well have thought herself neglected and ill-used by his goings on and could have done much to thwart him. And yet when the crisis arrives she immediately comes back into her own at the foot of the cross and accepts the infant Church (how incredible seeming at that moment!) as her new charge, as continuation and fulfillment of her first charge from God, and she is the Apostles' strength up to Pentecost, and so beyond.

In all of this what do we see? Complete, instant and lovingly confident response to the word of God whether communicated by an angel, her husband, her relations, kings, shepherds, innkeepers or her own Son. She asks nothing for herself, yet does not shrink from her responsibilities. And finally she is *there*: she holds, she sustains, she accepts. She is the Tower of Ivory, the Morning Star and Gate of Heaven: the battlers' Vision and the world's Reply. She is wholly free and yet her choices (though momentous) were seemingly few, and the right way not always obvious to one with less clear vision. (Surely it would be understandable to make a fuss about coming to birth in a stable? About emigrating to Egypt at one hour's notice on the

strength of a dream? About finding one's twelve-
year-old son after three days on the loose?)
Always she gives of her secure totality, and it
is secure and total simply because of her love
and her faith and her hope. Power, says Saint
Thomas (*I Contra Gentiles*, 70), is not called slight
because it can deal with slight things, but because
it is limited by them. How narrow was the gate of
free service by which Mary stepped into heaven
—to be crowned its Queen.

My soul magnifies the Lord,
my spirit rejoices in God my saviour;
so tenderly has he looked upon his servant,
humble as she is.
For from this day forth
all generations will count me blessed,
so wonderfully has he dealt with me,
the Lord, the mighty one.
His name is holy,
his mercy sure from generation to generation
towards those who fear him;
the deeds of his arm disclose his might.
The arrogant of heart and mind he has put to rout,
torn powers from their thrones
but lifted up the humble.
The hungry he has satisfied with good things,
the rich sent empty away.
He has ranged himself on the side of Israel his
     servant;
firm in his promise to our fathers,
he has not forgotten to show mercy
to Abraham and his children for ever.

O Lord Jesus Christ, to know you is to live, serving you is to reign. Grant therefore to us your faithful that we have the power to recognize your face, and to serve all your needs in all whom we meet, and that so we may all come together with you into the Kingdom prepared by your Father, where with your mother you already live and reign for ever.

10 Giving Up and Saying Goodbye

IT HAS BEEN SAID that middle age consists of learning the art of saying Goodbye, for as the years accumulate all else can seem to depart, decay or die. And I suppose it was in some part with this in mind that Yeats said: "Our souls are love, and therefore a perpetual farewell." But let us always remember that the word Goodbye derives from the phrase God be with you. For then we will rest assured that that to which we say Goodbye is simply going to God, and as we saw earlier with the Resurrection, nothing is lost, but everything finds its ultimate home in God; a home in which we will have our share amid the many mansions (Jn. 14:2).

So when we say Goodbye we give something up to God. Life is simply the opportunity to give. Life comes from God's desire to give, his wholly untrammeled generosity, and from this all life should take its character. The essence of giving is that we do not lose by the gift. To what a treasure house, therefore, are we heirs! Anything that is ours is so by gift, and because of our divine image and likeness we have it in our power to continue and to enhance that gift right up to the final and all embracing gift of our whole selves at death. And all before that is practice for that tremendous adventure.

We are told to love God, and sometimes we query how this can be done. But remember that God *is* love, and *is* life, and therefore any and all experience of these two is an experience of God, and God of himself cannot cease to live or to love or to give. And therefore we can say that there is a sense (it is not the whole truth, but it is a true *sense*) in which we have not made the most of anything until we have given it to God and said Goodbye to it. Up to that moment it is only *ours*, by right of possession. It is not possessed by the Creator and all of creation. If we clutch and hold on for our own little private selves it is lost, and so are we. If we give, all gain.

There is the story of the rich Russian lady who on her death was buried in hell (to her great indignation) and who complained so loudly to Saint Peter in the heavens above that he looked down and asked the cause of this commotion. When she told him, with some bitterness, how important she was and how clear a right she had by birth and breeding to be in heaven he asked her a simple question: "Did you ever give anything away without hope or expectation of a return?" And there was a long pause while she thought. Then she replied in triumph that once in the town of Omsk she had given an onion to a beggar. So a great search was instituted in heaven where all gifts must come in the end, and sure enough it was found eventually. So Saint Peter tied it to a rope and lowered it into the pit of hell so that the lady might hold onto it and be drawn out. She grasped it firmly, and there seemed a good chance that it would be strong enough to get her out. But as she began slowly to rise above the others who were damned, they saw in her their own chance of escape, and all those near her held onto her so that they might go up with her, and those who could not reach her held onto those who did, but with the weight of them all it began to look dangerously as if the onion could not take the strain and that if they did not let go the lady would not be saved, and as this was her only gift, and therefore her only and last chance of salvation, she cried out in righteous indignation to all of them in hell: "Let go: it is *my* onion, not yours!" and immediately the onion slipped from heaven's rope and she sank back grasping firmly the one thing she had ever really said Goodbye to.*

We cannot grow if we do not give. This we must look to spontaneously in all the world around us so that we do all in our power to fulfill the needs and possibilities we see. But also we

---

*A parable must not be pressed too closely over all its details (witness the unjust steward), so if we must apologize for too crude a picture of hell and of the economy of salvation, let us at the same time acknowledge the paramount importance of pure generosity without hope of return.

need to put a positive act of our loving will into what seems to be taken from us, realizing that God is showing his love and his trust as much (if not more) in his immediate taking back as in his original giving. And if our heart seems to be bound up in that which now God is taking from our possession, why then it runs all the closer to God, in whose heart is our only rest.

Therefore when friends leave us for the ends of the earth, and we feel that perhaps we shall not see their face again, like the Ephesians with Saint Paul (Acts 20:38), our sorrow at that immediate loss must be swallowed up in the realization that as our hearts have gone with them so is our life now enriched with all of their new life, and they are like ships of merchandise which can but return with gain a hundredfold for all who love. And in this way Death is but the supreme journey.

So also with all the powers and skills and strengths that have grown up within us from the day of our birth—our Beauty that must die: let us not regret their passing, but rejoice at their everlasting fulfillment in that land which is the inheritance of God's beloved children.

Our Lord himself on his last night on earth with his friends told them so clearly that it was better for them that he should go (Jn. 16:7) for otherwise they would remain enthralled by his limited bodily presence, and growth would be at an end.

But with the Resurrection, and death swallowed up in victory (1 Cor. 15:54), our inheritance expands to take the breath away: *all* that you and I experience can be a part of heaven's treasure house. So do not fail to bring the passing sunset and children's laughter with you, and love's sorrow at departure. All can be gained if given up with a true Goodbye.

A Tender Farewell to the World

Must I then leave you, deep woods that overhang slow rivers and pastures in between? Must I leave you also, small ancient cities of delight, multiple, filled with a traditional glory, exhibiting in a hundred corners of carved stone the delight my fellows before me had in the business of this world and in the spirit of their province and in the humour of coming and going, of leaving and of arriving, of the market?

Must I leave you, too, strong debates of mind with mind and bolting out of truth; conversations of men?

Must I leave you also, most noble of certamina, the encounter with the sea? Must I never more communicate through the tiller with the life of the hull and with the God that is in the wind upon the sail, nor hold her any more into the exultant water, nor any more make with a fixed gaze for the mark far away upon the headland over the edge of the world: that headland that might be a low cloud save that it does not move: that headland behind which are the stone piers and the sheltered water and the roofs of home?

Must I leave you, innumerable records of men, and my own poor delight—but delight—in addition thereto; the written word and the silent sound of it in the mind, the rhythm of English and the idea taking on form and being?

It is said that all companionships are grevious to lose, and that while all good things must end, of all good things the hardest to abandon are the intimate companionships of the soul, books made or making.

When I have read the writings of some man long dead, a great poet or a master satirist proclaiming the glory of God, my mind has taken on an amplitude to which it seems hardly native; I grew beyond my boundaries, I became by communion a part of that which I received, and thenceforward I moved, not a companion of, nor even an heir to, but a very participant in, the epics and the feasts, the discoveries, the attitudes, the revelations of so great a company. One might marvel how man ever achieved so much by letters and could so multiply and extend himself and spread outwards into perpetual new fields of achievement. If we have been of the poets and of the prophets in this fashion, can we bear to be rid of that magnitude—must we say, even to that, goodbye?

And our own verses, our own delight in expression concluded and in the accomplished magic, must that also be left aside, put away, abandoned?

The greater mountains, wherein sublimity so much excels our daily things, that in their presence experience dissolves, and we seem to enter upon a kind of eternity—must so much majesty be relinquished, and must we turn back from it and go away ungratefully as from lords to whom we have grown disloyal? Must we have done for ever with those immeasurable deeps into which vastness we were by our littleness absorbed? Must I no more catch my breath at seeing, revealed beyond the clouds above me, a living spear of light which was the suddenly apparent ice of the summit? Are the mountain paths never again to be known by me and that approximation to the heavens?

But must I leave you also, best things of all, which are the clothing and extension of the soul itself, the things of home; the walls and the roof and the furniture of man's life? You, my habitations... must I leave you, fields all about, and most familiar slopes low and far against the southern sky? Must I leave you, mundane fulfillment?

Yes, now we must say goodbye. And yet, all that tremendous experience (from which I am sprung) awaits me and awaits us all as but one tiny particle, one infinitesimal facet, of the whole delirious revelation of Paradise to which we all are called, to which we shall return.

Dear God, your generosity has been from

without beginning and can have no end; so in that generosity we pray you to give us the vision and the power to make of all we have and are one great gift that you may be our All in all, and that we may grow to the immensity of that gift.

11 Past, Present and Future

GOD IS ETERNAL. This means that he is all-at-once. There is no past from which he comes, no future to which he goes. If there were change in him his perfection could not be complete: either it was there and is now no longer, or it is not yet, and is to come. He lives eternally and perfectly in the unchanging Now.

With us, in a finite creation, it is very different. For us there is movement and change, and time, which is their measure. Our present is always moving and can sometimes seem to be no more than the uneasy and insecure link between past and future.

But as with God (whose image and likeness we carry through all our existence) our reality is in the present. And yet how often we try to escape it!

Of course we are built up out of our past and *are* our past, and a man without memory is maimed indeed. But the past, and our memory of it, only has significance insofar as it relates to the present, gives us a grasp and understanding of ourselves here and now. Always we are being launched into the virgin future, and only from the present can that adventure come.

It did not require Job or Solomon to tell us that the burden of living is a harsh one indeed, and when the pressure gets too much we can fly away from reality by a great many paths, all with their element of fantasy. But it has perhaps needed the psychologists to tell us plainly that every flight from reality takes its toll of the spirit. Such flights always leave us the poorer, less open to the true demands of reality. "If I drink oblivion of a day," wrote Meredith in his fearful poem on Modern Love, "so shorten I the stature of my soul."

Simple dreaming and fantasy is so clearly a debilitating escape, if it becomes our whole life, that it needs little demolishing in our present context, but the flight into the past or future perhaps requires rather more attention.

For widows, especially, there can be the lure of memory and the past: to live in the happy days gone by, when all was secure and fulfilled and well. "Those were the days: if only they could return. Those are the only times worth thinking about. Nothing now has any meaning or point."

But these are ghosts, they can give us nothing except an even greater dis-ease in the present (which will still continue knocking on our door, and getting us out of bed and presenting us with worries and concerns). Of course they were real, and have added something of reality to us, but they are subject to the law of diminishing returns, and if they are now *all* our life then we are adding nothing to what we are or can be. All God's presents are being spurned, his plan of love is blunted. We are homeless.

The future is a little different, for we must plan and foresee (and use our memory of past experience in doing so). But again the danger is making our future everything: "When I get that legacy; when I get married again; when I can retire; when the children are educated...." This has the advantage that it often keeps us active and occupied. But what an impoverishment for ourselves and for all around us if the present gives us nothing: that future will become a rainbow, never reached, the achievement will come at such cost to present living that we will find it too strange and uncomfortable a land to live in when it becomes the present reality.

These three strands of our life must be bound together: only so can we achieve the perfection and fulfillment of God's Now.

Time that anticipates eternities
And has an art to resurrect the rose;
Time, whose lost siren song at evening blows
With sun-flushed cloud shoreward on toppling
    seas;
Time, arched by planets lonely in the vast

Sadness that darkens with the fall of day;
Time, unexplored Elysium; and the grey
Death-shadow'd pyramid that we name the past—
Magnanimous Time, patient with man's vain
   glory;
Ambition's road; Lethe's awaited guest;
Time, hearkener to the stumbling passionate story
Of human failure humanly confessed;
Time, on whose stair we dream our hopes of
   heaven,
Help us to judge ourselves, and so be shriven.

                                Siegfried Sassoon

The years:
The passing years.
How their constancy succeeds.
Movement is not all,
But the still silence
Needs movement around it
For its own understanding.
To be still amid the passing
Is to pass as well.
Prayer moves,
For God is passing good.

Still voice upon the Mountain:
   let me hear you.
Dear presence in the Cloud:
   I will not fear you.
All at once Eternity:
   I am: I will be near you.

12 Dread

THE DEVIL IS ALWAYS trying to get us out of the present, where, as we have seen, our reality lies, and one of his most effective weapons is dread: an unease about the future. He makes a lot of hay in that field, and does an impressive amount of destructive work in our garden of the present as a result.

Dread is very different from fear. Fear is the very real and present reaction to the threat of danger. Like all human emotions it can be experienced to excess, and in excess it can paralyze or inspire very harmful and irrational decisions. But it is a clear and definite emotion which we have all experienced, cannot expect always to avoid, and which we control by controlling our reactions to it. But dread is a much more vague and ill-defined thing, and for that reason all the more damaging in its results and all the more difficult to grapple with. And yet it rests much more with our will whether it is to thrive or not: it is the difference between anger and sulking or a harbored resentment. In it we create our own torture chamber, our own hell, and only our own wills can set us free.

Of course there is the need for prudence and foresight: we must look to what is likely to happen, and take steps accordingly. But either there is something to be done—as with the young monk I knew who lay awake one morning and said: "If that alarm clock doesn't go off pretty soon I am afraid I am going to be late for matins," or there is nothing to be done—as with the story of Saint Philip Neri playing cards with some companions. The conversation got round to death, and they were asking what each would do if he knew he were going to die within the hour, and one said he would go to confession, and another that he would go to the church to pray, and a third that he would try to be reconciled with his greatest enemy. But Saint Philip said that he would continue to play cards, for he was ready to die, and there was no formless dread in him.

When the Proverb-maker says that the fear of the poor is their poverty (10:15) he is really talking about dread, that hopeless feeling of no defense. And hopeless is the word: for hope is the answer to this paralyzing vice.

Now hope is not a facile optimism in the face of expectation and reality: it is the fruit of faith. It is the confidence that God loves his own and cannot abandon them; it is the conviction that nothing can separate us from the love of God (Rom. 8:39); it is the will to work always to forward the creative purpose of God.

When we feel the defenses down; when life seems pointless or blank; when the future stretches before us as a dead plain or a menacing threat, then we need to remember Abraham (Gn. 12:1) who was called by God from the safe comfort of his father's home in Haran out into the desert and to an unknown land that God in his own time would show him. And from Abraham's response comes all the adventure and triumph of the chosen people and our salvation. This was what Our Lord meant when he said he who would keep his life will lose it, and only he who is prepared to lose his life will find it (Mt. 10:39).

I remember when I was a child during the war how we had some chickens that roosted in a tree by night. And once there came a fox and settled down beneath them, watching them quietly with his beady eyes. All those chickens were safely out of his reach, and they were just as safe before his arrival as after it: they had slept up there for months without mishap and could confidently expect to continue so. But the old fox went on watching them quietly with his beady eyes. If he had jumped up, or barked at them, or snapped his jaws they might have had some reason for fear and could have recognized it and coped with it. But no: he only went on watching them quietly with his beady eyes. And dread began to invade them. What was going to happen? What would he do? What should *they* do? And they began to cluck and to shuffle about on their perch. And

as they got more excited, and made more noise,
and began to flap their wings the old fox was
watching them quietly with his beady eyes.
The commotion got louder and more furious as
the chickens got an even clearer and more awful
picture of their fate if they were to fall off their
perch, and the stillness of the old fox continued,
watching them quietly with his beady eyes. And
eventually, of course, it was too much for one of
those chickens, and with great flapping and
squawkings it fluttered down to its untimely end,
killed by its own created dread.

Let it not be so with us.

Strong God which made the topmost stars
    To circulate and keep their course.
Remember me, whom all the bars
    Of sense and dreadful fate enforce.

Above me in your heights and tall
    Impassable the summits freeze.
Below the haunted waters call
    Impassable beyond the trees.

I hunger and I have no bread.
    My gourd is empty of the wine.
Surely the footsteps of the dead
    Are shuffling softly close to mine!

It darkens. I have lost the ford.
    There is a change on all things made.
The rocks have evil faces, Lord,
    And I am awfully afraid.

Remember me: the Voids of Hell
    Expand enormous all around.
Strong friend of souls, Emmanuel,
    Redeem me from accursed ground.

The long descent of wasted days,
    To these at last have led me down;
Remember that I filled with praise
The meaningless and doubtful ways
    That lead to an eternal town.

I challenged and I kept the Faith,
    The bleeding path alone I trod;
It darkens. Stand about my wraith,
    And harbour me—almighty God.

Hilaire Belloc

Lord, you have chained the Devil down and he is powerless to harm me if I do not let him; in your mercy therefore free me from the chains and prisons of my own making and his suggestion, where baseless dread can keep me so long and so far from the joy of your freedom and life.

13   Suffering

SO MUCH OF THIS little book seems to have been about suffering in one form or another, that perhaps it would be a good thing to try and gather together the different thoughts on the subject that have been running through it.

Genesis tells us that suffering and death came into the world as a result of sin (Chap. 3), and although the connection is not always immediately clear the Old Testament does draw out with relentless persistence the consequences of this. But with the New Testament something quite differenct appears: remember Our Lord being asked by the disciples whether the man born blind suffered this infirmity on account of his own sins or those of his parents (Jn. 9), and his reply that it was neither, but that the works of God might be made manifest in him. Not that he himself denied the connection, as witness his telling the man cured at the pool of Bethsaida to sin no more, lest worse befell him (Jn. 5:14).

Suffering, therefore, is not *simply* a punishment, but rather the context of God's creative act. If we are to grow it is going to hurt simply because we are (as it were) stretching our limbs, moving out from our warm homes, finding the new achievement uncomfortable—when we learn something really new it usually feels at first as though we had lost something, as we pass from the old, secure pattern.

But of course there is more to pain and suffering than that. There is the whole problem (typified by the blind man) of 'innocent' suffering: of children starved and tortured, of accidents and bereavements, of mental disorder and man's deliberate cruelty. All this seems utterly wasteful and pointless, and goes far in so many cases to persuade people that an all loving and all powerful God clearly cannot exist.

But God's answer in fact is to come into this arena of suffering himself, and thereby to change its whole meaning. He, the wholly innocent, the completely and creatively good, now makes of suffering a positive act. The Cross is not put upon his unwilling shoulders, but rather he comes forward to take it up. But he is the living and creative principle of the World; he is our life and our love. The Passion, therefore, has made pain and suffering relevant in quite a different way: they are now all part of a triumphant process which is brought together in the life of Our Lord. I think of two parallel images: there is the story that a Chinese student saw in Cambridge the rowing eights training on the river, straining every muscle, sweating under the abuse and imprecations of their coxes, looking as though pushed beyond the limits of endurance; and what was his comment? "I did not know that you still had galley slaves in England." Indeed, they were suffering physically all that galley slaves suffered, and yet a whole kingdom, a whole life, separated the experiences of those undergraduates from galley slaves. Then again, when I have watched those same young rowers in the Boat Race, when the race is over it is always the winners who are in better shape: the achievement of victory has confirmed them and swallowed up their pain, and yet they, in actual fact, must have expended more effort than those they defeated. So now with us: Christ's victory swallows up our pains, and all our innocent suffering is but a confirmation of God's love for his creation. We are filling up what is still wanting in the sufferings of Christ (Col. 1:24). *Everything* can now be turned into the life of the Resurrection. And this is not morbid: this is triumph. The martyrs went singing to their death. Nothing can hurt them: *all* is gain.

So often people try to persuade us that pain is unhappiness. But this is not so, if we do not let it be so. Unhappiness comes when the pain is not seen in any real context (for then it could be avoidable), or else it is when we want incompatible things (for that is to destroy all order, and we are back in our meaningless hell). Unhappiness is in the will. I remember reading the account of the airman Douglas Bader who lost both his legs in a crash and was lying in hospital, and all the pain had gone from him, and he felt as though he was gently floating away into a sweet haze. Then he heard two nurses talking outside the half-closed door of his room, and one was saying that he would not live through to the morning. And with that his attitude quite changed and he made a violent effort of the will, determined now to live, and to resist this gentle ebb of his life. And immediately his body began to feel pain, and the more he struggled for life, and worked his way back from that beguiling dream of death, the more pain flooded into his body and did its work, every wave confirming his will and his power to live.

This then is the Christian victory: that pain and suffering are never a dead loss. They are a share in God's life as it advances through his creation; they are a measure of that life, and are in no way to be considered worthy of comparison with the glory that is to be revealed to us (Rom. 8:18-23), and after we have suffered a little while the God of all grace, who has called us to his eternal glory in Christ, will restore, establish and strengthen us (1 Pt. 5:10). Indeed we have been called to innocent suffering (1 Pt. 2:21), even as God's servant has come to his afflicted Church to suffer with her (Is. 53).

Pain can be defined as the awareness of frustration (just as evil is the lack of, or destruction of, the good), and if this is so we can see how in the end it is irrelevant to ultimate reality and fulfillment. For when God is all in all, then all reality will be filled up and nothing will be lacking, and we will be able to see with Julian of Norwich how all will be well, and we will not say: "Lord, if it had been thus it would have been well," but "Lord, it is thus and it is well, and blessed mayst thou be."

> He was despised and rejected by men;
> a man of sorrows and acquainted with grief;
> and as one from whom men hide their faces
> he was despised, and we esteemed him not.
> Surely he has borne our griefs
> and carried our sorrows;
> yet we esteemed him stricken,
> smitten by God, and afflicted.
> But he was wounded for our transgressions,
> he was bruised for our iniquities;
> upon him was the chastisement that made us
>   whole,
> and with his stripes we are healed.
> All we like sheep have gone astray;
> we have turned every one to his own way;
> and the Lord has laid on him
> the iniquity of us all.
> He was oppressed and he was afflicted,
> yet he opened not his mouth;
> like a lamb that is led to the slaughter,
> and like a sheep that before its shearers is dumb,
> so he opened not his mouth.

Yet it was the will of the Lord to bruise him;
he has put him to grief;
when he makes himself an offering for sin,
he shall see his offspring, he shall prolong his days;
by his knowledge shall the righteous one, my
    servant,
make many to be accounted righteous;
and he shall bear their iniquities.
Therefore I will divide him a portion with the
    great,
and he shall divide the spoil with the strong;
because he poured out his soul to death,
and was numbered with the transgressors;
yet he bore the sin of many,
and made intercession for the transgressors.

Isaiah, 53

Lord, I confess that you are good, and that to you all gentleness and love belongs. And when there comes upon me the great pain of my heart and head, it is to you that I must look, and the look must be one of love, not reproach. If any should be reproachful it is you, who have stretched out your hands all the day, and I would not....

O Lord my God, I stand upright, when I should bow and kneel; how else can I learn but through the humbling discipline of pain?

Let me not forget that pain is our work, and the token which has the power of being honored in much gold. You have said that those you love you chastise—can it be that you love *me*? That cannot be—and yet it must be, for yours is the true love which stretches forth its hands all the day.

Lord, you would have me one with you. But if you and I can be one, then my pain is your pain, and since the pain is your love, why then it is my love too, and if I have your love when I feel your pain, then surely have I overcome the world.

O Lord, teach me gratitude, for I am yours.

14 Prayer

PRAYER IS THE raising of the heart and mind to God. Good. But the great trouble with the prayer of many of us is that it remains infantile: we are taught our prayers when we are very young in a few well tried formulas recited by our beds morning and evening, listened to by our mothers, and after that it becomes a personal and private affair which no one interferes with, and it is left at this infantile stage through lack of opportunity or desire or knowledge of how to develop it. But to leave our prayer at the nursery stage is as silly and as frustrating as to leave our language, interests, social intercourse, diet or reading at that stage: it is of vast importance to ourselves and to all around us that it should continue to be a living and developing thing. But unlike many other spheres of human activity the less we pray the less we feel the immediate desire or need to (in this it is like fresh air or exercise in a lot of people, and unlike eating), and fear and great tribulation are frequently the only causes that prompt people back to any sort of real prayer. But tribulation is obviously a very limited reaction in what should cover every movement of the soul. But even if limited, tribulation can be very genuine and very intense, and can be the root from which all else can spring.

If prayer starts from the realization of how vulnerable we are, or in what great need we stand, it can quickly grow to a realization of the power, the greatness and the love of God. And from there we can quickly come to his beauty. This is not an escape from the pains and burdens of our life, but rather it is making the incarnation true. As a result God lives more in his creation. Grace abounds.

Man cannot live properly by bread alone, or indeed by anything less than the Transcendent. And what does that mean, for heaven's sake?

It means that always we need to be going beyond what immediately we have achieved. God, we say, made everything, but is himself unmade. What is more, he made it all of nothing. Everything is made of nothing and God's word. But nothing has no part in God. God is in everything that is made, but is not limited by that thing. This universal law applies to ourselves and to all that we experience: always we should find our attention being taken beyond what we are meeting with: however great the depths within us, always there is the rainbow of God's creative action and life beckoning us on towards a horizon which is forever getting broader.

This is not always a pleasant process—any

more than living or loving can always be pleasant. For as we reach out to God we can feel, as it were, that we have touched him. But if we can contain God, then it is not God. To change the metaphor slightly, the bottom must always be falling out of our world if we are dealing in the ultimate reality of God. And this can be a fearful process, for it is a fearful thing to fall into the hands of the living God (Heb. 10:31).

And yet, the voices call and we needs must follow. God is our vision and our language and our ground. God is love, and therefore all that we experience of love *is* God. God is life, God is glory; God is the ordering and end of this world; God is joy; God is union; God is wisdom; God is strength; God is all goodness; God is courage in adversity; God is comfort in calamity; God is all generosity and the fulfillment of all desire; God is sweetness; God is light; God is food and drink; God is vision and hearing; God is beauty (and all beauty seen in men and women, sunsets or a flower should remind us of God); God is music; God is challenge; God is achievement; God is the ground of our being; God is the apex of our soul; God is our beginning and end; God IS.

When Moses talked with God on Mount Horeb God gave himself no name, simply saying that he was He Who Is. This is of vast significance. For once you are Zeus, then you are not Aphrodite; if your name is Mars you have the limitation of not being Juno. But the "God of Abraham, Isaac and Jacob" has no such limitation. All limited, finite existence comes from him and points to him, but he is not limited by it. The theologians (for whom we must have great sympathy and love, even as we must love all men) say that all things stand in relation to God, but that God does not stand in relation to anything. That is great food for prayer.

But how then should we pray? I do not think that Our Lord's answer to the disciples was meant to be a quick formula to be recited in half a minute. Rather it was a short litany of attitudes and areas of contact with God almost every word of which gives inspiration for raising the heart and mind. For if God is our father (not just yours or mine), then *all* men are brothers: he is our source of whom our earthly parents are but the model and image (for God is our mother also before ever Mary was). All our being comes from him through the urgency of his outpouring love; he takes us by the hand; he teaches us, rears us, corrects us; has a plan for us; loves us, and is proud of us. And not just for you and me who know each other already, but all mankind and all creation. He makes our home, and dwells in it himself, having furnished it with all the wealth that Genesis describes and that the Party political manifestoes promise. We bear his image. Our life is ours to grow ever closer to him in likeness, and to work for him and in his presence and with all the family, in his many mansions. Though when the six days of the new week are passed it will be for us all to rest together in his garden of delight (whose Greek name is Paradise). For heaven is his dwelling place, if the earth is his footstool, and always he is calling us to this existence whose fullness is his and to which he has made us heirs by a will written in his blood.

His name is holy. One. Complete. Everlasting. Ineffable. And yet within the one there is Trinity: Procession and the interchange of love: that Gift between Father and Son that is also called the Spirit.

God is beyond all words, save that which became flesh and dwelt among us. Before all else God IS. And God is holy. Here, in his name is all contemplation, here is all rest. Movement is secondary. Here is the One: the many are silenced. All praise, honor and glory here find their home.

Indeed he is in heaven, but he is not only Father, he is King also, and here is movement from within the stillness, for his kingdom must be spread throughout the world. A kingdom of justice, peace and love, and since the Resurrection *we*, his children, are the means whereby this kingdom must come, must spread throughout the world. And when that kingdom comes (by his power, but with us, even *us*, to forward it) it will be swept up into glory and his will shall be

confirmed and done in every particular. But
before that Day, that great Day when the stubble
is burnt and the true gold remains (1 Cor. 3:13),
his will must be forwarded and done as far as in
us lies in every particular. Within ourselves
first—and how much room for thought there is
here as we measure up our failings and refusals
and denials, and see the more of this the more
clearly we see his own name and its holiness:
earth has such an infinity to climb to reach even
to Heaven's Gate, let alone its summit. But so far
beyond our petty selves stretches the infinite
world in all its complexity, finding no rest until it
finds its rest in its true father, until its doings are
ordered as his will is done in heaven.

Only now do we come to petition, and hardly is
the word "Give" out of our mouth before we are
taken on to "Forgive," and so to temptation and
evil, those last arrivals in the Garden, and the
first to disappear when the Seraphim puts up his
fiery sword.

Prayer must almost always start with words as
with almost all entry into love (and prayer is but
the expression and flowering of our love affair
with God), but, as also with love, words are not
all: there is listening and there is looking and just
being in the presence of the beloved. All these
should play their part, and indeed an increasing
part. And as we grow older this also should grow.

When we are young we are like a dashing mountain stream: all bubbles and leaping laughter; fresh from our spring we rejoice in the light; we chatter round rocks, we cascade into pools, we know each little trout and stickleback that has fought his way so far; sheep are our only companions, and lonely men who walk the hills; the clouds (who are our fathers) come down to kiss us as we lie in the arms of our mothers the hills. But when we get down to the plains we are channeled and embanked, work mills and water the fields; we are bridged and fished and foster villages and then towns. And finally there is that period when we begin to smell a different air, we rise and fall by a force no longer from within us: we have met the tide, and soon we are carried out beyond our little selves into the deep broad bosom of the sea. So also with our prayers: after the chatter of youth and the great work of the middle years, then he for whom we are destined gives us our rise and fall, our ebb and flow, making our own, with increasing understanding and realization, the prayers of Our Lord's last day on earth: Not my will but thine be done: Forgive them: Into thy hands I commend my spirit. And if we follow this pattern we also shall thirst (even though the chalice is not taken from us), we also shall feel the cold dry wind of desolation as the sun no longer gives its light, and we feel abandoned by our God. But if we continue to the end we also will be able to say with him: It is consummated. And on that day we shall be with him in Paradise.

In the end Prayer is everything: it is love's expression and fulfillment. And in the evening God will question us on love. Nothing else remains. Prayer is not the preserve of monks and nuns: they may be the experts (though even this is far from being a universal truth) and in the second half of life—as most of those to whom this book is addressed will be—there is death to be reached out for with less of distraction, more of quiet purpose. Here prayer can flourish if we have but the will.

Other men's prayers abound: the best and most tried are the psalms. Books on prayer abound: Brother Laurence on the practice of the presence of God, Francis de Sales' *Introduction to the Devout Life*, the Works of Saint Teresa the Great of Avila, the *Cloud of Unknowing*, the *Revelations of Divine Love* by Dame Julian of Norwich, the Works of St. John of the Cross, the Spiritual Maxims of Pere Grou or his book on *How to Pray*, Hubert van Zeller's *Moments of Light*, the Spiritual Letters of Abbot Chapman, *The One Who Listens* by Michael Hollings and Etta Gullick. But only use what helps *you*.

Remember also that discretion is the mother of the virtues, and that in this journey we cannot always go alone, that there can be much darkness, dryness and doubt, that the devil can disguise himself as an angel of light, and that therefore at times we need someone to hold us by the hand, to give us an objective judgment on where we are and how we progress. This is what is meant by a Spiritual Director, and this is what confession should increasingly be about: having someone to aid us in the pursuit of self knowledge. Not just cleaning up our sins, but helping us to judge the value of our actions and experiences, steadying in doubt, confirming in right judgment, sharing in joy and illumination; embodying the principle that we are never alone, nor our lives simply our own. God is incarnate in his Church. The Communion of Saints resides in us.

Half Way

The start is numbness,
a gentle unease beyond all grasping.
There is no touch,
even the wind is still
and the warm rain
negative.

Pain would be preferable:
Painfully life can be felt;
it is the first brave assertion,
stepping out from self-engrossed imprisonment.
Over the wall:
what there?
"Nothing," say those who fall back
into the deadening, soft enclosure.

But some scramble over and away
into the fearful unknown,
abandoning the mapmakers' conclusions
exactly arrived at.
For them the brambles
and the rain now lashing cold;
hunger and fear in the darkness,
but somehow company and a direction,
if only outwards
from that dead centre.

And I am there
suddenly in the midst of them.

  What now?
Where are the points of reference?
Will there be eating or sleeping on the way?
Is this dark depth pregnant with new world?
  Who can tell:
  Let us accept direction with agnosticism.

But I:
I am taken;
taken by the hand,
a hand rough from the hard work of discovery
and the thing achieved.

There is possibility.
Heights rear up
and the demand intolerable.
Up that sheer side?
Faith in so frail a thread?
Think what can now be lost!
Can I not hoard my scrupulous treasures,
picked up along a swift road's passage?

And settle
for no more possibility?

No:
Once more up and away
and the few lights' delight
soon lost.
Mist now,
and the ever crushing weight
of sheer height
achieved at rasping cost:
the air asserts its brutal ascendency.
Breath becomes all.
And yet,
beyond breath
is the ascent, still calling.
The mist thinning and receding.
Can there be view?
Can there be vision?
Arrival?
Richness given and received?

Achievement is possibility:
Meeting is imminent.

And, dear God,
—still going—
I am glad I went.

15 Joy

WHY DID GOD make you? asked the catechism of my youth, and gave (to me) a very inadequate answer. Of course we must learn to know, love and serve God in this world, and should be happy with him hereafter. But this seems to imply that all the jam is tomorrow. No: God made us because he loved us and because he wanted us. And because he wanted us to share in his life, his life of pure joy. And that life is with us now. Jesus said that he came that we might have life and have it more abundantly (Jn. 10:10). And if we keep his commandments we abide in his love, and his joy will be in us and our joy will be full (Jn. 15:10).

Joy is a duty. And if you think that makes a poor picture of joy, I think it makes a fine picture of duty. Duty simply means the guidelines to joy: duty has, in the end, no other object than to bring us to bliss, and for all that the path to bliss may on occasion be hard, let us not forget Jacob's seven years work for Rachel made light for the joy of her (Gn. 29:20).

Note this also: that to him who has, more is given. The joy of the Saints no man can take from them, and through the life of God within them (which is what Grace is), they turn all around them into yet more life, and therefore joy of life goes with them and all around them. Joy is the essential state for it is the state of God. Listen to what Aristotle could say three hundred years before Our Lord, and there were few men drier than Aristotle when it came to putting down the facts of life whether human or divine: "The life of the first principle (upon which depends the whole universe and the world of nature) is like the best which we temporarily enjoy. It must be in that state always, since its actuality is also pleasure. ... If then the happiness which God always enjoys is as great as that which we enjoy sometimes, it is marvelous; and if it is greater it is still more marvelous. And yet this is the case" (Metaphysics, 12.7).

Our joy rests in this, that we have been given the secret of this world: we have the Way, the Truth and the Life, and the Truth has set us free (Jn. 8:32). Of course we can still feel frightened, and hurt and abandoned and depressed, and we are not called upon to grin and laugh through it all. Cheerfulness is largely a matter of temperament and can be a deal too hectic and off-putting on occasion. No: Saint Paul tells the Philippians again and again to rejoice, though he adds that all men should also see their modesty and forbearance. And his reason for this joy? That the Lord is close to us. Nay, he is in us: it is not our little puny lives by which we live now but his life in us (Gal. 2:20), and nothing can come between us and the love of Christ, even if we are troubled or worried or persecuted or lacking clothes or food. For these are the trials through which we triumph by the power of him who loves us. And neither life nor death, no angel or prince, nothing that exists now or that is still to come, nor any power or height or depth or any created thing can come between us and the love of God (Rom. 8). And that is why Julian of Norwich tells us that God wants us to rejoice more in God's whole love than to sorrow over our own failings for "it is the most worship to him of anything that we may do that we live gladly and merrily for his love." Indeed a troubled or dejected spirit will never love God perfectly, nor do much good to his honor, and a joyous heart is more easily made perfect than one that is cast down.

So this again is where the Saints have it all their own way (and for heaven's sake let us all be Saints, *now*, and not have all this miserable waiting about): *everything* except sin alone is an arm for good—and even sin when it is past and recognized and repented: think of Saint Peter and Judas, and their two reactions to betrayal. If we make no mistakes we make nothing. Think of all that mess in the kitchen before the banquet is served (though once it is served, it will go on for ever, so worry not for the washing up, and everyone comes in for the banquet, except for those who were invited and refused).

Joy should bubble up and burst its banks always; it cannot be held alone: even the angels had to sing out their joy to the shepherds. And God had to create simply because he could not keep his secret to himself. And all things can be turned to good: look at the supreme irony of the serpent's prophecies. Indeed we shall be as gods (Gn. 3:5), because once it was seen to be expedient that one man should die that the whole nation should not perish (Jn. 11:49) our glory was assured.

Let not our desires be narrow, for God plans to fill us to the utmost of our yearnings, and to beyond all that heart and mind can conceive (1 Cor. 2:9). This world is our nursery, and here we must grow and so extend here and now our capacity to give and to receive all love and all joy that they may be at their uttermost for that home towards which we now all journey in such glorious company.

Oh the Beauty and the Glory and the wordless Wonder.

> Though our mouth were filled with song like the sea,
> And our tongue with music like the rumbling of its waves,

And our lips with praise like the open spaces of
    the sky,
And our eyes were bright like the sun and the
    moon,
And our hands outstretched like the eagles of
    heaven,
And our feet were fleet like the hind's—
Still we should not suffice to thank thee,
O Lord our God, and the God of our fathers,
And to bless thy name
For one of the thousand-thousand thousands of
    thousands
And myriads of myriads
Of good occasions which thou didst confer
Upon our fathers and on us.

Haggadah: before the drinking of
the fourth cup

When the Lord restored the fortunes of Zion
we were like those who dream.
Then our mouth was filled with laughter,
and our tongue with shouts of joy:
then they said among the nations,
"The Lord has done great things for them."
The Lord has done great things for us;
we are glad.
Restore our fortunes, O Lord,
like the watercourses in the Negeb.
May those who sow in tears
reap with shouts of joy!
He that goes forth weeping,
bearing the seed for sowing,
shall come home with shouts of joy,
bringing his sheaves with him.

Psalm 125